D0464047

Dinners in a Scottish Castle

From the very heart of the Scottish Highlands comes a new recipe book full of distinctly Scottish recipes from a great hostess.

The Lady Glentruim lives with her husband, Macpherson of Glentruim, a chieftain of the clan, in remote Glentruim Castle deep in Inverness-shire. The ancient castle of Glentruim was destroyed at the beginning of the last century and was replaced by the present solid granite pile, the greyness of which belies the warmth of its interior . . . and the splendour of its cuisine and hospitality.

Sandra Macpherson's cooking is renowned internationally and she has extensive experience of catering for large house parties. Her menus rely on what the land around provides in plenty—fish, fowl and game—and here are a selection of tasty yet easy to prepare dishes using venison, hare, grouse, pheasant, rabbit, salmon and lobster.

The Lady Glentruim presents here fifteen balanced dinner menus for a party of house guests staying for a fortnight together with recommendations for the leftovers and tips for the hostess.

An essential addition to the library of every hostess, here is a real taste of Scotland beautifully illustrated in colour.

Dinners in a Scottish Castle

The Lady Glentruim

Paul Harris Publishing

Edinburgh

First published 1983 by
Paul Harris Publishing
40 York Place
Edinburgh

ISBN 0 86228 078 8

Printed and bound in Scotland by
Spectrum Printing Company, Edinburgh

Menus

1. Scallops of the West
   Glentruim Venison
   Eagle's Nest

   Creamed Potatoes
   Baked Carrots
   Fried Cabbage

2. Piper's Spinach Soup
   Citrus Pheasant
   Laird's Favourite

   Roast Potatoes
   Green Beans
   Courgettes

3. Shellfish in Aspic
   The Glorious Twelfth
   Castle Cake

   Mashed Potatoes
   Brussel Sprouts
   Peas

4. Haddock Mousse
   The Monarch of the Glen
   Morning Dew

   New Potatoes
   Fried Onion Rings
   Green Salad

5. Chieftain's Onion Soup
   Invernahavon Rabbit
   Brandy Snap Baskets

   Croquette Potatoes
   Broccoli
   Green Beans

6. Loch Carron Crab
   Breakachy Hare
   Whisky Creams

   Creamed Potatoes
   Cauliflower in White Sauce
   Kidney Beans

7. Soup of the Fields
   Coraldie Duck
   Pearl in the Oyster

   Roast Potatoes
   Spinach
   Baby Carrots

8. Shrimp Pancakes
   Dish for the Stalker
   Prince's Crown

   Baked Potatoes
   Green Cabbage
   Boiled Beetroot

9. Mint Tomatoes
   Harvester
   Cairngorm Ice

   Boiled Potatoes
   Cauliflower in Batter
   Peas

10. Truim Salmon Cheese
    Venison Craigdhubh
    Island in the Mist

    Mashed Potatoes
    Marrow in White Sauce
    Green Cabbage

11. Skye Prawns
    October Pheasant
    Gaelic Pancakes

    Roast Potatoes
    Mushrooms
    Broccoli

12. Orange and Tomato Soup
    Spey Salmon Steaks
    Blackberry Whorl

    Creamed Potatoes
    Peas
    Tomato Salad

13. Ghillie's Trout
    Rabbit in Tarragon
    Strawberry Tower

    Rice
    Skinned Tomatoes
    Green Beans

14. Coast Mussels   Parsely Potatoes
    Highland Stew   Spinach
    The Ladies Orchard   Mashed Turnip

15. Chicken Liver Pâté   Fried Potatoes
    Summer Isles Lobster   Sweetcorn and Peppers
    Liqueur Truffles   Green Salad

Introduction

"There is a strange wild place called Glentruim on the left hand going North". So wrote Lord Cockburn, the High Court Judge, in his diaries as the coach took him on his Circuit journey from Edinburgh to Inverness. That was a century and a half ago and in so many ways his words still hold true today. Much else changes but in this lost, lonely and lovely world of the Scottish Highlands the old traditions live on.

Before a dinner party all the guests assemble in the drawing room and talk and laugh with the distant and haunting sound of the Piper playing the music of long ago in the hall outside. Some do not notice when the music stops but then there is the heavy sound of the great gong summoning guests to the dining table. The sound of the pipes starts again and the Piper entering the drawing room silences all conversation.

When I first came to live in my husband's home, I noted a curious tradition. As the Piper walks through the room it is the privilege of the Laird, as host, to choose the most attractive lady guest and to offer her his arm as the Piper leads them into the dining room. It is, however, then the privilege of his Lady to choose the most attractive man to follow her husband, and the other male guests then follow with their own choice of partner. But they cannot choose—no matter how attractive—their own wives! In the dining room the Piper proceeds down the whole length of the long table and up the other side and the Laird, upon reaching his own place at the head of the table, stops and places his chosen lady on his right. In the same way the hostess at the bottom of the table stops and places her chosen partner on her right. Each gentleman then follows holding the chair for his chosen partner.

It is a very old and curious tradition—how old I do not know—but because of it each person at the dining table finds themselves in company which they enjoy. It is, in my view, a far better way of seating guests than by trying to decide who would like to sit next to who and then rather arbitrarily allocating names to each place.

When all are seated the sound of the pipes dies away. Then there is silence and a quiet interval before the hum of conversation starts again. In that quiet moment, the candlelight flickers and my heart sinks. The success of all dinner parties depends so much on the careful and thoughtful preparation of food. I ask myself, "Have I remembered this?" "Did I do that correctly?". It is a moment that every housewife entertaining guests in every home in every country will recognise as all too familiar. I look up the table of polished oak with its glasses, its shining silver and candlelight. I sense the air of expectancy among my guests and again I feel that moment of uncertainty.

As one course follows another all doubts ebb away amidst the laughter and talk and enjoyment of the friends who have come to our home. As each course begins there is again a hushed moment of anticipation as the first mouthful is savoured and then the talk and laughter begin again. At every dinner party there is a threshold point when I know from the faces of my guests and the atmosphere that my dinner party has been a success.

Even now, after many years, having entertained at my table princes, princesses, politicians and my husband's closest friends, there is still no dinner party at which I as hostess do not experience, albeit briefly, that moment of uncertainty. I now know that that moment of uncertainty will always remain. It will always be there to spur me on to think of new and better ways to prepare and present food.

At the close of dinner a message passes from my husband's eyes to mine with a quiet smile. It is a message of thanks and a signal that as hostess I should rise. As I do all others stand, each gentleman holds back the chair of his partner and all the ladies retire to the drawing room to leave the gentlemen alone. We talk quietly together but our conversation is interrupted by the laughter from the menfolk we have left behind in the dining room as they sit with port and brandy in the wide and generous company of men together. Later they join us and again there is silence. The logs glow and spark in the white marble fireplace. My fingers at first gently touch the strings of the *clarsach* and then more confidently the chords ring out. In this way all the lovely Gaelic songs, many of them hundreds of years old, are heard again and loved again.

I often think that half the battle of cooking for a dinner party is over once the menu has been decided. When guests are staying for a week or more, not only does the hostess wish to cook something special but also she wants variety for her guests. It can sometimes be a strain, especially in the second week, to have to conjure up different menus. How often I have heard a tired hostess say, "What on earth will I give them to eat tonight!" Also, it must not be forgotten that cooking is not the only job of the day, and when guests are in the house, even though they may be "helpful relatives", work is still inevitable. For this reason, I thought I would put together a book of my menus to attempt to relieve the busy hostess of a little of the work load.

In cooking for a dinner party one is aiming to have a meal that not only looks superb, but tastes delicious as well with, I may add, as little work as possible! When one is called upon to entertain during the day, it is not possible to spend the whole day in the kitchen. With this thought in mind, the reader will notice that in my menus the starters and sweets are, more often than not, cold. I do this as much as possible because these items can be prepared in advance, thus allowing me more time with my guests. It is particularly convenient if you are having guests staying for a few days at a time, as quite a few of the dishes in this book can be prepared on a "quiet afternoon" (with luck!).

I have placed the menus in order for a fifteen day stay, selecting as varied a choice as possible to ensure guests are not bored. I attempt to start and finish each meal with something I feel is that little bit special to tempt the palate and—vary the main course.

Not all the menus given in this book may be to the particular liking of everyone, especially where game is involved, and an alternative meat may be used.

While the recipes are laid out in menu fashion, these, of course may be used according to the taste and choice of the individual and need not necessarily be served as shown. The menu plan is simply a suggestion for planned dinners to assist the busy hostess to balance her courses and avoid too heavy or too light a meal.

I now confess that in the early days of my marriage I could cook nothing and employed a professional chef who did not please my husband's palate. When I started cooking on my own, my husband on tasting the first mouthful would often look up at me and say "How did you make that?" Not knowing how to cook and not following any recipe books, I could only reply to him "I made it out of my head" and so I dedicate this book to the most severe critic of all my culinary endeavours—my dear husband.

May I wish you, the reader, *'Bon Appetit'* and hope you will enjoy trying some of the recipes I use for our guests at Glentruim.

Sandra Macpherson of Glentruim
Glentruim
May 1983

Acknowledgements

I am indebted to Mrs. Vivienne Haddow who typed the manuscript. Without her constant encouragement this book would never have been written.

I am further indebted to Carolyn Ann, coutourier, who created the dresses which I have worn on so many memorable occasions.

My thanks also to George Cocker for his superb photographs of the dishes I created, as well as the cover photographs. The photograph of myself and my husband at Glentruim Castle is courtesy of Douglas Corrance and the Scottish Tourist Board.

Menu One

Many people are unaware that the west coast of Scotland with its sandy beaches and wild and rugged coastline extends to nearly a thousand miles, and beyond that coastline are nearly a thousand islands. It is one of the most forgotten and unknown parts of all Western Europe. Along its shores there is a treasure of sea-food, much of which is exported to hotels and restaurants in Europe and America. It has a flavour entirely its own derived directly from the turbulent and restless North Atlantic seas.

Scallops of the West

Glentruim Venison
Creamed Potatoes
Baked Carrots
Fried Cabbage

Eagle's Nest

Suggested Wine for Main Course:
Chateauneuf-du-Pape (Rhone Red)

Scallops of the West

1 lb of scallops
1 tablespoon of white wine
1 tablespoon salt
2 oz fried bread crumbs

Sauce

½ lemon
2 oz flour
2 oz butter or margarine
½ pint milk
seasoning to taste

Method

Melt butter and briskly stir in flour. Add milk gradually, making a thick white sauce. Add to the sauce seasoning and juice of lemon.

While making sauce, put about 2 pints of water in a saucepan and bring to the boil. Add salt and white wine. Keep water boiling, then drop in scallops and bring back to the boil for 1 minute. Strain and fold scallops into prepared sauce.

Serve in individual dishes and garnish with fried bread crumbs. If scallop dishes are used, pipe edges with mashed potatoes and sprinkle paprika on top. Serve with home made bread.

Glentruim Venison

3-4 lb piece of haunch of venison
1 clove garlic
½ teaspoon fine herbs
2 oz beef or lamb dripping

cranberry sauce
2 tablespoons red wine
1 tablespoon gravy powder
1 tablespoon red currant jelly
seasoning to taste

Method

Smear dripping over joint. Season with salt and pepper, crushed garlic and fine herbs. Place in centre of pre-heated oven at 400°F. After 15 minutes turn down to 325°F, cover joint with foil and cook for roughly 40 minutes per lb (baste from time to time). Joint is ready when tested with skewer; if no blood or water seeps out it is done. Remove from oven. Carve fairly thick and place in oven-proof dish. Use all the juice in the baking tray to make a rich gravy with wine, gravy powder and redcurrant jelly. Pour over meat and keep warm until ready to serve.

Serve with Cranberry Sauce

Eagle's Nest

4 egg whites
2 pinches cream of tartar
10 oz. castor sugar
  (sieved)
2 dessertspoon of
  cornflour

1 teaspoon vanilla
  essence
1 pint double cream
½ lb. cherries
2 teaspoon Kirsch.

Method

Whip egg whites until stiff. Add one third of the sugar and the cream of tartar and whisk again. Add another one third and whisk. Fold in the remainder of the sugar, the cornflour and vanilla essence.

Spoon half the mixture onto a greased baking sheet, making as many small meringues as possible. With the remaining mixture, pipe a flat circular base on a greased baking sheet. Bake both mixtures in a pre-heated oven at 275° for about 1½ hours until meringue is hard on top and bottom.

Chop cherries (saving a few) remove stones, whip the cream and mix together with fruit adding the Kirsch. Pile the cream mixture onto the meringue base and place the small meringues around the fruit and cream making a nest. Decorate with remaining fruit.

Menu Two

The playing of the pipes is an essential part of a Highland dinner party. The bagpipes are known throughout the world as part of the tradition of Scotland. There is no other instrument which has led men into battle and given them such courage to fight and win, but which also can create nostalgia a feeling of longing and epitomise moments of sadness.

Piper's Spinach Soup

Citrus Pheasant
Roast Potatoes
Green Beans
Courgettes

Laird's Favourite

Suggested Wine for Main Course:
Sancerre (Loire White)

Piper's Spinach Soup

1 lb spinach
1 small onion (chopped)
2 oz. butter or margarine
1 pint chicken stock
¼ pint double cream
seasoning to taste

Method

Melt butter in pan and gently fry onion, add spinach simmer for 5 minutes. Pour in stock, season to taste and cover. Simmer again for one hour. Cool slightly. Liquidise (or put through sieve) and put back in pot ready to heat up when required. Garnish each bowl with a tablespoon of cream.

Serve with home made bread.

Citrus Pheasant

2 plump pheasants	¾ lb. oatmeal
2 oz. fat	¼ lb. suet
2 tablespoons cream	rhind and juice of
½ teaspoon fine herbs	orange
seasoning to taste	rhind of ½ lemon

Method

Pre-heat oven to 375°F. Mix together oatmeal, suet and grated rhind of orange and lemon. Then add ½ of the fine herbs and seasoning. Stuff pheasants with the mixture, smear fat over the birds and season. Place in the pre-heated oven in a roasting tin for 10 minutes; reduce to 350°F and cover with tin foil. Allow to cook for about 40 minutes, removing the foil for the last 10 minutes.

Lift pheasants from roasting tin and keep warm. From juices of the pheasants remove a little of the fat and make a rich sauce adding the juice of the orange, and finally stir in the cream. Pour half over the pheasants before serving and serve the remainder at table.

The Laird's Favourite

24 squares of cooking chocolate
 4 eggs (1 egg per 6 squares chocolate)
 1 tablespoon water
 2 oz. butter
 1 teaspoon brandy or rum (optional)
¼ pint double cream

Method

Melt chocolate with water and butter over a pan of hot water. Separate eggs and whip the whites until stiff. When the chocolate is melted, remove from heat and stir in beaten egg yolks and alcohol if used. Fold in egg whites and pour in bowl or individual dishes. Place in a cool place to set. Decorate with whipped double cream.

**The Lady Glentruim and her husband,
MacPherson of Glentruim,
at home, Glentruim Castle**

Menu One
**Glentruim Venison
and Scallops of the West**

Menu Two
Citrus Pheasant

Menu Three
Shellfish in Aspic

Menu Three

The Glorious Twelfth is known throughout the world as the day when the season for grouse shooting begins. The expression started in Scotland and dates from early Victorian times when grouse shooting first became popular. Highland heather-clad hills teem with grouse in Summer, and then later in the Autumn the dominant males take their territory and drive off all others which join in packs and, for want of feeding, die in the winter snows. For the shooter, grouse shooting means many miles of walking over heather moor and peat bog. For the gourmet, it means a dish beyond all others.

Shellfish in Aspic

The Glorious Twelfth
Mashed Potatoes
Brussel Sprouts
Peas

Castle Cake

Suggested Wine for Main Course:
Gervrey Chambertin (Burgundy Red)

Shellfish in Aspic

½ lb. shelled prawns	½ red pepper
½ lb. prawns in the shell	½ green pepper
½ lb. mussels	¼ pint sherry or white
2 pkts aspic jelly (2 pints)	wine
1 lemon	1¾ pints warm water

Method

First prepare the aspic jelly—dissolve aspic in warm water and the sherry or white wine, simmer until clear then leave to cool. Cut two round slices off each of the peppers and chop remainder. When aspic is cool, pour ½ inch into the mould and leave to set. Decorate the first layer in the way you wish it to be seen when turned out. In this recipe, I had the round slices of peppers filled with shelled prawns and decorated with mussels. Cover with aspic and leave to set. Continue adding remaining shellfish and peppers and covering with layers of aspic until all is used up. Place in fridge to set. As it takes a bit of time for the aspic to set, between layers, you can prepare some of the other courses while waiting.

When dish is turned out, decorate it with the prawns in the shell and lemon wedges. Serve with home made bread and mayonnaise.

To turn out—dip dish in hot water for two seconds, then using your thumbs, lightly press down all along the edges to loosen, then turn out. If it does not turn out immediately, tap the bottom and give it a gentle shake. Repeat process if necessary.

The Glorious Twelfth

3 grouse
6 pieces home made bread cut thick and fried
6 pieces of bacon
½ onion (chopped)
1 bay leaf
2 oz. margarine
½ teaspoon mixed herbs

1 tablespoon cornflour
1 tablespoon water
2 tablespoons cream
1 tablespoon red wine
¾ pint stock
2 oz. grated carrots
2 oz fried breadcrumbs.
seasoning

Method

Cut grouse in half and cut away back-bone which is not needed. Melt margarine in pan and fry onions. Add grouse pieces and fry on both sides. Season and add stock, mixed herbs and bay leaf. Simmer gently for 2 hours.

When tender place grouse pieces on top of fried bread on serving dish. Fry bacon and place under or on top of each piece of grouse and put in oven at 400°F for 10 minutes before serving. Remove bay leaf from stock and thicken with cornflour and water, add wine and cream. Pour some of the gravy over the grouse to moisten, serve remainder at table. Decorate with grated carrot and serve with fried bread crumbs.

Castle Cake

3 oz. plain flour
3 oz. castor sugar
3 eggs
½ lb. raspberries
1 pint cream

2 sherry glasses of concentrated orange juice
2 sherry glasses of orange liqueur

Method

Line and grease two 7" tins. Sift flour. Whisk eggs for 2 or 3 minutes. Add sugar and whisk eggs again until pale. Fold in flour. Place in tins and bake at 350°F for about 20 minutes. Cool on rack. Place one of the layers on a plate and pour over it half the orange juice and half the liqueur. Cover with whipped cream. Place other layer of sponge on top and pour over remaining juice and liqueur. Decorate with whipped cream and fruit.

Menu Four

The Monarch of the Glen is the title of an immortal painting by Landseer. Every Highland gamekeeper has been searching for that same stag on his land, and that stag has never been found again. Nevertheless, throughout the Highlands, the population of red deer has been increasing. They have adapted to the change in the environment with the loss of woodlands over the last centuries and now live and thrive in arctic conditions, where many other creatures would perish. Thus they are arguably the most proud and independent living creatures in our land.

Haddock Mousse

The Monarch of the Glen
New Potatoes
Fried Onion Rings
Green Salad

Morning Dew

Suggested Wine for Main Course:
Côtes du Rhone (Rhone Red)

Haddock Mousse

1 lb. haddock
½ small onion
3 cloves
3 peppercorns
1 bay leaf
½ pint milk

2 tablespoons lemon juice
1 dessertspoon of gelatine dissolved in
3 dessertspoons of hot water

2 oz. butter
2 tablespoons flour
½ pint cream
1 tablespoon mayonnaise
seasoning to taste

1 dessertspoon tomato
  puree
few drops tabasco
1 lettuce
½ red pepper

Method

Put cloves into onion and place in pan with milk, peppercorns, bay leaf and fish. Simmer gently for 20 minutes. Remove bay leaf, peppercorns and onion. Melt butter in pan and mix in flour, strain fish, pour milk into flour and butter, gradually, making a sauce. Add lemon juice and seasoning. Pound mixture together, with the fish, adding cream and the gelatine, or put all into liquidizer. Pour into well greased mould and place in fridge to set. This will take about 2 hours. Turn out and decorate with lettuce and red peppers. Mix together the mayonnaise, puree and tabasco and serve this sauce and home made bread with the mousse.

The Monarch of the Glen

4 venison steaks cut 1
  inch thick
2 oz. butter
1 clove garlic (crushed)
4 tablespoons marsala
seasoning to taste

½ lb. chicken liver pâté*
1 dessertspoon cornflour
4 thick slices brown
  bread
¼ pint double cream
watercress
redcurrant jelly

* See Recipe for Chicken Liver Pâté given in Menu No. 15.

Method

Spread garlic and half the butter over steaks and season. Place remaining butter in frying pan and melt. Add steaks and begin to fry gently. Pour marsala over steaks and cover. Simmer gently for approximately 10 minutes, turning steaks once or twice during cooking. When steaks are cooked according to preference, remove from pan and place on top of the prepared bread which has been first spread with a thick layer of pâté. Bread and steaks should be placed on a hot dish and kept warm. Take cornflour with 2 dessert-spoons of water and mix to a paste, then add slowly to pan simmering until sauce thickens. Remove from heat and stir in cream. Pour some of the sauce over steaks and garnish with cress. Serve remaining sauce and red currant jelly at table.

Morning Dew

3 egg whites
4 oz. castor sugar
   (sieved)
juice of ½ lemon
2 teaspoons Drambuie

½ pint cream
homemade lemon
   biscuits

Method

Whip egg whites until very stiff, add half the sugar and whisk stiff again. Repeat with remaining sugar. Fold in the lemon juice and Drambuie. Put into oven-proof dish in a preheated oven at 300°F for 30 mintues. Should be golden on top when ready. Serve immediately with whipped cream and lemon biscuits.

Menu Five

Almost seven hundred years ago in the fields of Invernahavon, below Glentruim Castle, our ancestors fought a battle against a neighbouring clan, and being refused the honour of having the right hand flank in battle, they withdrew with their clansmen to nearby hills and watched the battle being fought below them. When their allies were in danger of defeat, they drew their swords and put the enemy to flight. Now in this century the battle field is a place with gentle rivers murmuring quietly of memories past.

Chieftain's Onion Soup

Invernahavon Rabbit
Croquette Potatoes
Broccolli
Green Beans

Brandy Snap Baskets

Suggested Wine for Main Course:
St. Julien (Bordeaux Red)

Chieftain's Onion Soup

2 lbs onions
2 oz. margarine
2 pints beef stock
2 oz grated cheddar cheese
seasoning to taste

Method

Slice onions thinly and fry gently in margarine until cooked. Add beef stock and bring to the boil, simmer for 1 hour. Season to taste. Grate cheese over top and serve with home made bread.

Invernahavon Rabbit

Legs of 3 large rabbits
3 oz firm cream cheese
4 oz fresh bread crumbs
1 egg
2 oz margarine or butter
½ teaspoon fine herbs
½ teaspoon salt
¼ teaspoon black pepper
juice of ½ lemon

Sauce

¼ lb mushrooms, chopped
½ small onion, chopped
2 oz butter
2 oz flour
¼ pint white wine
2 tablespoons cream

Garnish

½ lemon
water cress

Method

Remove meat from bone in as large pieces as possible and flatten with a mallet. Using meat off each leg, spread one piece of meat with cheese and cover over with another. Fill all the meat in this way. Sprinkle over all the pieces the seasoning, herbs and lemon juice. Dip pieces into beaten egg and cover with bread crumbs. Fry gently in margarine until cooked, turning frequently. Keep warm in ovenproof dish. Decorate with cress and remaining lemon.

Sauce

Melt butter in pan and fry onion and mushrooms until cooked. Stir in the flour mixed with a little water and gradually add wine. Remove from heat, season to taste and add cream.

Brandy Snap Baskets

2 oz self-raising flour
2 oz sugar
2 oz margarine
2 tablespoons syrup
½ teaspoon ginger
1 teaspoon brandy

Decoration

2 peaches halved and skinned (fresh if possible)
4 cherries
¼ pint cream

Method

Melt sugar, syrup and margarine. Remove from heat and add remaining ingredients. Mix well.

Grease and flour baking tray. Place four spoonfuls well spread out on sheet and bake for about 8 minutes in oven pre-heated to 350°F. When golden in colour, take out and let cool for a few seconds until they can be lifted off tray.

Grease bottom of glass (shape of which can hold half peach).

Lift brandy snaps off tray and wrap around bottom of glass, then put on rack to cool.

Repeat procedure until you have required number.

Place cool baskets on serving dish. Put half peach into each one. Decorate with cream and cherries.

When 4 baskets are made, you can make ordinary brandy snaps. Shape these by wrapping them around a wooden spoon. Fill with cream when cold. These look very attractive arranged on the serving dish along with the brandy snap baskets.

Menu Six

Breakachy is a lovely stone-built house from the last century. Its name however was well known in olden times since there lived there, many centuries past, the Macphersons of Breakachy, a branch of Cluny Macpherson the clan chief. The present house overlooks the Upper Spey Valley, a broad and fertile valley surrounded by rugged mountains whose far place give birth to the River Spey. In Springtime in the early morning the grassy fields of Breakachy deep in dew, and bathed in sunlight, are the home of the brown hare savouring the freshness of early summer.

Loch Carron Crab

Breakachy Hare
Creamed Potatoes
Cauliflower in White Sauce
Kidney Beans

Whisky Creams

Suggested Wine for Main Course:
Hermitage (Rhone Red)

Loch Carron Crab

1 lb fresh crab meat	seasoning
2 slices white bread	paprika
2 tablespoons homemade mayonnaise	1 lettuce
	1 tomato
1 lemon	parsley

Method

Separate white meat from brown meat. Make bread crumbs with the slices of bread and mix these with the white meat and mayonnaise. Season and add this mixture in the centre of a serving dish on top of lettuce leaves and surround it with the brown meat. Squeeze half the lemon over the crab and sprinkle paprika on top. Decorate with parsley, slices of remaining lemon and tomato and serve with brown bread and butter.

Breakachy Hare

2 hare	2 oz margarine
1 onion	2 oz seasoned flour
½ pint beef stock	2 oz cornflour
½ red pepper	2 fl. oz water
½ green pepper	2 tablespoons red wine
1 tablespoon redcurrant	seasoning
jelly	

Method

Cut hare into pieces discarding any bones with little flesh. Chop onion and half of the peppers and fry; add hare joints dipped in seasoned flour. Brown on all sides. Add stock and simmer for about 2 hours until tender. When cooked, place hare joints onto serving dish. Thicken stock with cornflour and water. Add wine and redcurrant jelly. Season to taste. Pour over hare and decorate dish with remaining peppers.

Whisky Creams

12 homemade lemon
    biscuits
½ pint cream
1 teaspoon whisky
2 oz walnuts

Method

Whip cream and chop walnuts as small as possible saving four for decoration. Fold chopped walnuts and whisky into cream. Place four biscuits on ashette and cover with cream mixture. Repeat procedure and place remaining biscuits on top. Pipe rest of cream over top and sides completely covering biscuits. Place walnuts on top. This should be made at least one hour before serving.

Menu Seven

Coraldie now is merely a line of stones showing where once was the old croft house. There in the last century families lived and worked, and below by the quiet waters of the Spey, there is a pond where ducks flight in, in the late evening as they did then. The croft house and the people have gone with the economic change brought about by the industrial revolution in the last century and not by the greed of land-owners as some would have us believe. In the twentieth century it would be difficult to make a living from the few barren acres, but it is not difficult to remember the people who once lived there, and whose children's children are still the game-keepers and shepherds whose mannered gentleness is so much a part of the Highland way of life.

Soup of the Fields

Coraldie Duck
Roast Potatoes
Spinach
Baby Carrots

Pearl in the Oyster

Suggested Wine for Main Course:
Nuits St Georges (Burgundy Red)

Soup of the Fields

½ lb mushrooms
1 small onion
4 oz margarine
1 pint chicken stock

2 oz flour
seasoning
½ pint milk

Method

Chop onion and fry in 2 oz of margarine until cooked. Add chopped mushrooms and fry gently for five minutes. Add stock and simmer for three quarters of an hour. Melt remaining margarine and stir in flour. Put this mixture plus soup through liquidizer, adding seasoning and milk. Heat through when required. If you do not have a liquidizer make sure the onions and mushrooms are chopped into small pieces before cooking. Make white sauce with margarine, flour and milk and gradually add it to the stock.

Coraldie Duck

2 ducks
2 oz fat
1 tablespoon brandy
2 tablespoons redcurrant jelly
seasoning

1 orange (juice and shredded peel)
1 dessertspoon tomato puree
2 tablespoons red wine
1 tablespoon gravy powder mixed with
1 tablespoon water

Garnish

1 orange
spinach

Method

Pre-heat oven to 350°F. Smear ducks with fat and season. Roast in oven for about one and three quarter hours. When cooked, remove from oven and cut in half taking out back-bone. Place on serving dish and keep warm. From the roasting tin, pour off most of fat leaving just a covering in the pan. Thicken with gravy powder and water and add all other ingredients. Pour half this sauce over the duck and decorate with orange segments and spinach. Serve remaining sauce at table.

Pearl in the Oyster

Choux Pastry

3 oz margarine
8 oz water
4 oz flour
2 large eggs (use largest size)

¼ pint cream.
8 oz dark dessert chocolate
3 drops peppermint essence

Method

Melt the margarine with water and bring to the boil. Take off heat and add sieved flour—beat. Cook slightly then beat in eggs, one at a time. Spoon on to dampened baking sheet in small balls. Bake at 400°F for fifteen minutes. Prick sides and leave on rack to cool.

Melt chocolate over heat and stir in peppermint essence. Open out each pastry in half and coat insides with chocolate and leave to set. Whip cream and pipe a pearl on each half. Serve with remaining cream.

Menu Eight

The deer stalker is a gamekeeper who spends his life in the high hills and the lonely places of heather-clad mountains. Perhaps one of the best known and best loved stalkers in recent times was Mr. Angie Bain. He was a man of infinite kindness and gentleness, who loved the mountains and the deer that roamed on them. Like other stalkers he was happy and free in a way which people who live their lives in the valleys can never be. Since he died, his name has become a legend. He died as he had always wished, among the hills where like his father, and his father before him, he had lived and laboured.

Shrimp Pancakes

Dish for the Stalker
Baked Potatoes
Green Cabbage
Boiled Beetroot

Prince's Crown

Suggested Wine for Main Course:
Chateauneuf-du-Pape (Rhone Red)

Shrimp Pancakes

Pancakes

4 oz plain flour
1 egg
½ pint milk

¼ teaspoon salt
2 oz margarine

Menu Four
The Monarch of the Glen

Menu Five
Brandy Snap Baskets

Menu Six
Loch Carron Crab

Menu Seven
Pearl in the Oyster

Filling

¼ lb shrimps	3 oz butter
2 oz mushrooms	1 teaspoon tomato puree
1 small onion	1 oz flour
1 lemon	2 tablespoons milk
	seasoning

Method—Pancakes

Sieve flour and salt. Mix in egg and gradually beat in milk. When mixture is ready, heat a little of the margarine in a frying pan and pour mixture to form a thin layer over the bottom of the pan. When brown underneath, turn and cook other side. Turn out on to greased paper and repeat procedure. Keep warm.

Method—Filling

Melt the butter in a pan and add chopped onion and chopped mushrooms. Fry until cooked. Stir in flour over low heat gradually adding the milk and tomato puree. Fold in the shrimps, season and place a little of the mixture into each rolled pancake. Serve with wedges of lemon.

Dish for the Stalker

4 lbs venison (approx.)	½ lb cranberries
2 oz butter	6 oz castor sugar
2 oz flour	

Marinade:

2 cloves	3 peppercorns
4 stick celery	1 bay leaf
1 carrot	pinch rosemary
1 onion	pinch oregano
1 clove garlic	1 tablespoon vinegar
¾ pint red wine	

Method

Chop vegetables and put all of marinade ingredients in china bowl. Place meat in the marinade and leave for 24 hours turning meat from time to time. Remove meat from marinade. Simmer marinade over heat until it reduces a little. Place meat in roasting tin and pour marinade back over it. Roast in pre-heated oven at 325°F and cook for about 40 minutes per lb.

Dissolve the sugar in a little water, add cranberries and simmer for 20 minutes. When the meat is cooked, remove from marinade and strain. Put marinade in a pan and reduce once more to half. Add ⅓ of the cranberries, thicken with flour and melted butter and pour some of the gravy over the roast. Serve remaining gravy and cranberries at table.

Prince's Crown

1 medium size melon	¼ lb black grapes
1 sherry glass of Drambuie	¼ lb green grapes
	1 lemon jelly
½ pint double cream	crystallised fruit (optional)

Method

Cut skin off melon and level the bottom. Then cut off the top and remove seeds. Scoop out a little of the melon into balls and tidy up the inside.

Wash and cut the grapes in half removing any seeds. Place the melon balls and a few of the grapes back into the melon. Prepare the jelly with only ¾ pint water plus the Drambuie. Pour this into melon and leave to set. Place top back on and pipe cream over whole of melon starting from the top. Decorate with remaining grapes and crystallised fruit if used and serve with remaining cream. This can be sliced at table.

Menu Nine

Cairngorm is the name of a mountain close by Aviemore which has in recent years become the centre of skiing in Britain. Apart from its reputation as a skiing centre, it is beloved as a place of wild and natural beauty known only to hill walkers, climbers and naturalists. Over its vast area no voice is heard except the roar of rutting deer and the strange wild call of the ptarmigan. In recent years reindeer have been introduced from Scandanavia and are now a flourishing population.

Mint Tomatoes

Harvester
Boiled Potatoes
Cauliflower in Batter
Peas

Cairngorm Ice

Suggested Wine for Main Course:
St Emilion (Boreaux Red)

Mint Tomatoes

4 large tomatoes
3 hard boiled eggs
seasoning

2 tablespoons homemade
mayonnaise
1 mint leaf chopped
finely

Method

Cut top off tomatoes and scoop out centres. Chop the hard boiled eggs and mix with mayonnaise and chopped mint. Season and put back in tomato. Serve on lettuce leaf and decorate with tomato tops.

Harvester

4 pigeons
1 onion
1 clove garlic
4 oz butter
pinch fine herbs
seasoning

2 oz flour
2 tablespoons cream
½ lb stoned cherries
   (save a few for garnish)
2 tablespoons red wine

Method

Cut out the pigeon breasts; fry chopped onion and garlic in half the butter then add the meat. To this, add cherries, the red wine, fine herbs and seasoning. Simmer until the pigeons are tender, for about 1 hour. Put pigeons into a serving dish. Thicken the sauce by adding it to flour mixed with the remaining butter and stir in the cream. Pour over the pigeons and serve.

Cairngorm Ice

4 Square pieces of
   sponge (see recipe 3
   and prepare   in one
   12" x 8" tin)
3 egg whites
4 oz castor sugar

Ice Cream

1 lb raspberries
1 pint double cream
2 oz sugar

Method

Ice Cream. (make this early in the day)
Put raspberries and sugar in pan and cook until sugar is melted, sieve then allow to cool. Whip cream and fold in puree. Freeze.

36

Prepare a meringue mixture by whisking egg whites until stiff, add half the sugar and whisk again. Repeat with remaining sugar.

Place pieces of sponge on baking tray. Place as much ice cream as possible on top. Cover each one with meringue mixture making sure all ice cream is sealed. Bake in a pre-heated oven at 400°F for about ten minutes. Should be golden brown on top when ready. This must be served immediately.

Menu Ten

Craigdhubh is translated from the Gaelic as the Black Rock. It is a steep mountain of grey furrowed cliffs and wind-torn cloud standing over Glentruim. For centuries past it has been the symbol of Clan Chattan and its name, the battle cry of the Clan. In 1746, the Clan Chief hid in a cave after the battle of Culloden and for nine years remained in hiding from the English Red-Coats until he escaped to France. In present times it has become the mecca of rock climbers from all over Britain, offering some of the best low level rock and ice climbing in Scotland.

Truim Salmon Cheese

Venison Craigdhubh
Mashed Potatoes
Marrow in White Sauce
Green Cabbage

Island in the Mist

Suggested Wine for Main Course:
Cotes du Rhone (Rhone Red)

Truim Salmon Cheese

½ lb cooked salmon
2 oz butter
½ teaspoon mustard
2 oz flour

approx. ½ pint milk
4 oz cheddar cheese
seasoning to taste

Method

Spread fish over oven-proof dish. Grate cheese. Melt

the butter in pan, add flour and make a sauce, gradually adding the milk. Add two thirds of the cheese, cook through and season with pepper, salt and mustard. Pour sauce over the fish and sprinkle remaining cheese on top. This can be popped into a hot oven fifteen minutes before being served.

Serve with home made bread or toast.

Venison Craigdhubh

roe venison haunch, (approx 3lbs boned)	8 oz soft margarine
12 oz plain flour	3 tablespoons water
½ teaspoon salt	1 cup red wine
½ lb fresh dates (stoned)	1 teaspoon mixed herbs
1 oz cornflour mixed with	1 clove garlic crushed
1 tablespoon water	seasoning to taste
1 tablespoon cream	parsley

Method

Place venison on greased baking tray, cover with wine, crushed garlic, mixed herbs and seasoning. Wrap the pastry over the top of joint and place in the middle of the oven at 325°F for two and a half hours. Garnish with chopped parsley and serve with venison gravy.

Pastry

Rub in margarine, water and half the flour plus salt. Fold remaining flour in and roll out to ½" thick.

Gravy

When roast is ready, lift from tin and make gravy by mixing into juice from the meat, the cornflour and water, and chopped dates. Stir in a tablespoon of cream and serve with the meat.

Island in the Mist

¼ lb wild strawberries or similar fruit
2 oz sugar
½ pint cream

Method

Stew fruit in a little water and add the sugar. Strain
and put fruit through a sieve. Whip the cream and
fold in the fruit puree. Serve in individual glasses.
Save one or two whole fruit for decoration.

Menu Eleven

The misty island of Skye is a place set apart from the rest of Britain by its romantic past and its present loveliness. In the midst of its lonely quiet mountains, man can become part of nature and find his true identity. Some years ago my husband wrote verses to try to translate this feeling into words:

Mountains my love are strong and proud
Whose naked shoulders lift above
The heavy rolling weight of cloud
I would I had such strength my love.

And when wet rock in sunlight gleams
Upon the face of bravest peaks
Then every drop in all their streams
Runs like tears down their cheeks.

When in long Summer days the sun
Has warmed their faces brown and light
Then all their streams in laughter run
And whisper quietly in the night.

If I should laugh, or I should cry,
Should whisper in darkness all my dreams
No different from the hills of Skye
Her mountains and her streams.

Skye Prawns

October Pheasant
Roast Potatoes
Mushrooms
Broccolli

Gaelic Pancakes

Suggested Wine for Main Course:
Meursault (Burgundy White)

Skye Prawns

1 lb king prawns or lobster tails
1 lemon

Sauce

¼ pint homemade mayonnaise
2 teaspoons tomato puree
4 drops paprika
1 tablespoon cream
seasoning to taste

Method

Mix all sauce ingredients together except for cream which is folded in last.

Drop prawns into boiling salted water and bring to the boil again for one and a half minutes. Remove from water and shell threequarters of them. Fold them into the prepared sauce and decorate with remaining whole prawns.

Serve with home made bread and wedges of lemon.

October Pheasant

2 pheasants	½ teaspoon black pepper
2 oz butter	½ teaspoon salt
1 oz glace cherries	2 bay leaves
(reserve a few for	2 onions
decoration)	4 cloves
1 oz flour	1 apple
1 tablespoon water	1 lemon
	1 teaspoon tomato puree

Method

Place cloves into onions and put into middle of pheasants with bay leaves. Spread butter and seasonings over pheasant and roast as in Menu No. 2. When cooked, remove from oven and cut pheasants in two and keep warm. Drain excess fat off the juices in roasting tin and with the flour mixed with water, thicken the gravy. Add all glacé cherries chopped, except for a few reserved for decoration, and stir for 1 minute. Pour some of the sauce over pheasant and decorate with remaining cherries and slices of apple dipped in lemon juice.

Serve remaining sauce at table.

This recipe can also be done with chicken pieces.

Gaelic Pancakes

4 oz plain flour
1 egg
½ pint milk
¼ teaspoon salt
2 oz margarine

2 oranges
2 lemons
2 oz castor sugar
1 tablespoon orange
   liqueur
2 tablespoons whisky

Method

Sieve flour and salt. Mix in egg and gradually beat in milk. When mixture is ready, heat a little of the margarine in a frying pan and pour mixture to form a thin layer over the bottom of the pan. When brown underneath, turn and cook other side. Turn out onto sugared paper and fold twice. Repeat procedure until all the batter is used. Place pancakes into oven-proof dish.

Heat juice from oranges and lemons and dissolve sugar. Remove from heat and stir in liqueur. Pour over pancakes.

Heat over flame before serving, add whisky and set alight if desired.

Menu Twelve

The River Spey is the fastest running river in Scotland. It wends its way past the storm-torn mountains and wild and lonely hills of the Central Highlands, through woodlands and meadows and finally to the rich green pastures at Spey Bay, where it enters the North Sea. It is a river renowned in history. The timber from the Scottish Highlands was transported down to the sea on its waters and taken south to London for drainage and building in the seventeenth century. Now the River Spey provides some of the finest salmon fishing in the whole of Scotland. Every Autumn the female fish are stripped of eggs which are carefully nurtured and the young placed back in the womb of the mother river. The Truim, a tributary of the Spey, receives almost a third of the total restocking.

 Orange and Tomato Soup

Spey Salmon Steaks
Creamed Potatoes
Peas
Tomato Salad

Blackberry Whorl

Suggested Wine for Main Course:
Puligny Montrachet (Burgundy White)

Orange and Tomato Soup

4 oranges
1 lb tomatoes
1 small onion
½ teaspoon mixed herbs
1 pint chicken stock
¼ pint cream

1 oz margarine
1 dessertspoon sugar
1 dessertspoon concen-
   trated orange juice
1 dessertspoon tomato
   puree
seasoning to taste

Method

Chop onion and fry in 1 oz of margarine. When cooked, add chopped, skinned tomatoes. (To skin tomatoes, drop into boiling water for a few seconds, then skin should peel off easily). Add juice of oranges and remaining ingredients with the exception of the cream. Simmer for 30 minutes. Liquidize or put through a sieve. This can be thickened with 1 oz margarine and 1 oz flour if necessary. Whip cream and put a spoonful on top before serving.

Spey Salmon Steaks

6 salmon steaks (allow 1
   per person and
   a couple extra)
2 lemons
4 oz butter
seasoning

½ teaspoon ground
   pepper
½ teaspoon mixed herbs
½ pint white wine
1 tablespoon cornflour
1 tablespoon cream
watercress

Method

Season steaks adding ground pepper and mixed herbs. Melt butter in a pan and add salmon steaks. Cook 1 minute on both sides, then pour over the wine and cover. Simmer gently for 10 minutes. Remove steaks and put in a dish. Mix cornflour with cream and stir into pan making a thick sauce. Pour over steaks and decorate with cress and wedges of lemon.

Blackberry Whorl

½ oz yeast
4 tablespoons warm milk
4 tablespoons warm water
8 oz plain flour
2 oz castor sugar
2 eggs
2 oz butter

pinch of salt
¼ pint rum
¾ pint water
¾ lb castor sugar
1 lb blackberries
½ pint double cream

Method

Sprinkle yeast on top of milk and water and leave for 10 minutes. Sieve flour, 2 oz sugar and salt and mix in beaten eggs and yeast. Place butter on top of mixture in little pieces, then cover with polythene. Let rise to double its size for about one hour in warm place. Remove polythene and add 2 oz of blackberries and knead well. Place in greased circular tin and let rise again to double its size.

Boil water, ¼ lb blackberries and ¾ lb castor sugar together until reduced to half, then add the rum. Pour half of this over cake while still warm then leave to cool. Fill centre with remaining blackberries, pour rest of syrup over dish and decorate with half the cream serving the remainder at table.

Menu Thirteen

"Ghillie" is the Scots term for a man whose work takes him to lochs set amidst mountains and beside the waters of mountain rivers to look after the fishing of the waters. One such man was Mr. Peter MacDonald, who worked at Glentruim and whose genial personality gave pleasure to all who knew him. Like all fishermen, he was a man of great patience and tolerance which are qualities essential in any good angler. On only one occasion were these qualities lost. He took a Countess, who was a guest at Glentruim, down to the river and behaved toward her with his normal courtesy and respect. However, after she had taken and lost two salmon, when a third fish took the lure, he was heard to shout: "Strike now—damn it woman—STRIKE!" This time the salmon was duly landed!

Ghillie's Trout

Rabbit in Tarragon
Rice
Skinned Tomatoes
Green Beans

Strawberry Tower

Suggested Wine for Main Course:
Margaux (Bordeaux Red)

Ghillie's Trout

4 trout (1 per person)
2 lemons
1 oz butter per fish
seasoning to taste
1 tomato

Sauce

½ cucumber
½ pint mayonnaise
½ teaspoon paprika
(liquidize above together)

Method

Gut fish and place in greased oven dish. Put dots of butter both inside and on top of fish. Season and squeeze a whole lemon over the top. Place in oven pre-heated to 325°F for 20 minutes.

Garnish with lemon and tomato and serve with home made bread and cucumber sauce.

Rabbit in Tarragon

2 large rabbits
1 onion
1 clove garlic
2 oz margarine
¼ pint stock
2 oz seasoned flour
2 slices green pepper
2 slices red pepper

White Sauce:

¾ pint milk
2 oz flour
2 oz margarine
2 teaspoons tarragon

Method

Cut rabbits into pieces and only use hind legs and saddle. (The rest can be used for stock.) Dip pieces into seasoned flour. Fry chopped onion and garlic in 2 oz margarine and add the rabbit pieces. Add stock and 1 teaspoon tarragon and simmer for 1 hour or until tender. Make a white sauce with flour margarine and milk. Add tarragon and season to taste. Remove the pieces of rabbit from the pot when cooked and put on

Menu Eight
Prince's Crown

Menu Nine
Harvester

Menu Ten
Truim Salmon Cheese

Menu Eleven
Skye Prawns

serving dish—cover with white sauce and garnish with red and green peppers. (rabbit can be removed from bone first if wished.)

Strawberry Tower

1 lb strawberries
4 oz castor sugar
1 pint double cream
4 pieces of sponge (see menu 3 and prepare in one 12" x 8" tin)

Method

Chop up half of the strawberries and sprinkle over the castor sugar. Crush together with a fork. Whip cream and fold in half to the mixture. Cut four pieces of sponge through the middle and fill each one with the strawberry and cream mixture. Decorate top and sides with remaining cream and strawberries.

Menu Fourteen

Since the time of Johnson the Highlands have tended to be regarded by the rest of Britain as a wild and primitive place of high mountains, deep valleys and lonely lochans and streams. This picture of the Highlands is still, even today, largely true, and there are few other unspoilt and lovely places in Western Europe untouched by the hand of man. It is these qualities which draw people from all over the world to visit the Scottish Highlands to enjoy its natural beauty and to come to know the people who live there.

Coast Mussels

Highland Stew
Parsley Potatoes
Spinach
Mashed Turnip

The Ladies Orchard

Suggested Wine for Main Course:
Chateau Neuf-du-Pape (Rhone Red)

Coast Mussels

1 lb mussels cooked
4 oz butter
2 oz breadcrumbs
4 tablespoons white wine
1 small onion
½ clove garlic
seasoning to taste

Method

Fry breadcrumbs in 2 oz butter and set aside. Fry choped onion and garlic in remaining butter. Place mussels, onion and garlic in shallow oven-proof dish and season, cover with wine and breadcrumbs. Heat in oven pre-set at 375°F for 15 minutes before serving.

Highland Stew

2-3 lb piece of venison	¼ oz butter
1 lb sliced mushrooms	½ teaspoon black pepper
½ onion chopped	salt to taste
1 crushed clove of garlic	1 oz flour mixed with
1 tablespoon cream	1 tablespoon water

Method

Cut venison into thick pieces, season with pepper and salt and fry in butter along with the onion and garlic for 5 minutes on each side. Put into an oven-proof dish and add mushrooms. Place in pre-heated oven at 325°F and cook gently for about an hour until tender. Remove pieces of meat from dish and thicken gravy with flour. Lift from heat and stir in cream. Pour back over the meat and garnish with cress.

The Ladies Orchard

4 large cooking apples	2 oz roasted almonds
2 oz castor sugar	(chopped)
1 oz butter	¾ pint cream
	pinch of nutmeg

Method

Core the apples and fill with sugar and a dot of

butter. Place in a pre-heated oven at 350° and bake for half to threequarter hour until cooked but firm.

Whip cream and fold in almonds and nutmeg. Fill centre of apples with this mixture and decorate with remainder. Serve immediately after adding the cream.

Menu Fifteen

The west coast of Scotland benefits from the warm tides of the Gulf Stream and it is for this reason that, in this most northerly part of Britain, palm trees can grow. It is invidious to consider one place more beautiful than another. But of all places in the West, certainly one of the most lovely is an area in the midst of emerald seas lying North of Ullapool called the Summer Isles. At the end of a summer day, when the sun sinks down into the sea beyond the Outer Hebrides, the Summer Isles gleam like precious gems in a royal crown.

Chicken Liver Pâté

Summer Isles Lobster
Fried Potatoes
Sweetcorn and Peppers
Green Salad

Liqueur Truffles

Suggested Wine for Main Course:
Pouilly Fuisse (Burgundy White)

Chicken Liver Paté

½ lb chicken livers
2 oz butter
2 tablespoons cream

1 tablespoon sherry
1 clove garlic
seasoning to taste

Method

Fry livers and chopped garlic gently in the butter until cooked. Season to taste. Remove from heat, add sherry, then pound or put through a liquidizer. Add the cream just before the end of mixing. Put into a dish and place in fridge to set. Serve in scoops on top of lettuce decorated with lemon.

Summer Isles Lobster

4 lobsters
2 tablespoons whipped
  cream
seasoning to taste

2 oz butter
3 oz flour
4 tablespoons white wine
2 lemons
paprika

Method

Remove lobster meat from the shell, dice and cover with juice from one lemon. Make a thick sauce with butter, flour and wine. Season and fold the lobster meat into this sauce, then add cream. Fill lobster shells with the mixture and sprinkle paprika on top.

Serve with lemon wedges and home made bread.

Liqueur Truffles

1 chocolate cake
¾ cup brandy
8 oz plain chocolate
1 oz butter

2 oz chocolate vermicelli
¼ pint cream
1 oz butter
1 tablespoon water

Method

Crumble cake and soak in brandy. Melt chocolate over heat with the butter and tablespoon water. Mix chocolate into cake and leave until firm. Shape into balls and roll in vermicelli. Serve with whipped cream.

Recipe for the Chocolate Cake

2 oz self-raising flour	3 oz castor sugar
2 oz cocoa	2 eggs
4 oz margarine	pinch of salt

Method

Sieve flour, cocoa and salt. Cream margarine and castor sugar together and add an egg with a little of the dry ingredients, a little at a time. Fold in remaining ingredients. Line and grease a cake tin and pour in mixture. Bake in pre-heated oven at 350°F for 30 minutes.

STEVENS' PATENT
SELF ACTING
FLOUR
FEEDER & DUSTER

STEVENS' PATENT
DOUGH MAKING MACHINE

Menu Twelve
Spey Salmon Steaks

Menu Thirteen
Strawberry Tower

Menu Fourteen
Coast Mussels

Menu Fifteen
Summer Isles Lobster

Leftovers

HARE

Hare and Mushrooms

¾ lb. cooked hare
¼ lb. mushrooms
1 onion
2 oz. margarine

2 oz. butter
seasoning to taste
pinch of paprika
2 lbs. cooked potatoes

Method

Chop the onions and slice the mushrooms. Fry in margarine until cooked. Mix this with the pieces of hare and put into an oven-proof dish. Season to taste. Slice the cooked potatoes and cover the dish completely. Put dots of butter over the potatoes then sprinkle with paprika. Put into a hot oven for 15 minutes before serving.

Hare Curry

¾ lb. cooked hare
1 onion
1 oz margarine
2 dessertspoons curry powder

¼ pint hare stock
1 apple
2 oz cashew nuts
2 dessertspoons cornflour

Method

Melt margarine and cook the chopped onion in this, add curry powder and stock or gravy from hare (if you have any). To this add pieces of meat and simmer for ½ hour. Thicken with cornflour. Stir in cashew nuts and slices of peeled apple. Serve on a bed of rice.

Hare Carraway

¾ lb cooked hare
½ lb cooked carrots

1 teaspoon carraway seeds
2 sticks celery

Method

Cut celery into small pieces, mix all ingredients together using gravy from the hare, and place into a casserole. This can be heated up when required.

Hare Macaroni

½ lb cooked hare
1 large skinned tomato
1 teaspoon paprika
freshly ground pepper

2 tablespoons sugar
2 oz grated cheese
1 lb cooked macaroni

Method

Mix together the hare and the tomato. Stir in paprika, sugar and freshly ground pepper. Put cooked macaroni in oven-proof dish, pour hare mixture on top and sprinkle with grated cheese. Put into hot oven 20 minutes before serving.

Hare and Bacon

½ lb. cooked hare
½ lb. bacon
baked potatoes

Method

Place hare in a shallow heat-proof dish and season. Cover the hare completely with rashers of bacon. Put this under the grill, allowing bacon to be cooked while the meat heats through. The fat from the bacon will flavour the meat. Serve with baked potatoes.

Hare and Aubergines

½ lb. cooked hare
¼ lb. mushrooms
1 onion
1 clove garlic
seasoning to taste
3 aubergines

2 oz grated parmesan cheese
2 tablespoons olive oil
2 tomatoes
1 tablespoon tomato puree
3 tablespoons stock

Method

Chop garlic and onion and fry gently in a little until cooked. Add chopped mushrooms and diced hare. Stir in tomato puree and stock. Season. Slice aubergines and fry in remaining oil. Place half of the aubergines in the bottom of a casserole and pour half of the hare mixture on top. Place the remaining slices of aubergines on top and then the rest of the hare. Cover with grated cheese and put into hot oven 15 minutes before serving.

PHEASANT

Pheasant and Mushrooms in a Nest

¾ lb. cooked pheasant   2 oz flour
¼ lb. mushrooms   seasoning to taste
½ onion   paprika
¼ pint milk   4 lbs potatoes
2 oz butter   2 oz grated cheese

Method

Chop onion and mushrooms and fry in butter. When cooked, stir in flour on very low heat, gradually add milk making a thick sauce. Cut pheasant into small pieces and stir into sauce. Season to taste. Having previously cooked the potatoes, mash these and make a large nest on a serving dish. Pour pheasant and mushrooms into the nest and shake a little paprika on top. Sprinkle grated cheese over the sides of the potato nest and pop into a hot oven for ten minutes before serving.

Pheasant Egg Curry

¾ lb. cooked pheasant   2 oz margarine
2 large or 3 small hard boiled   2 dessertspoons curry powder
    eggs   ¼ pint chicken stock
½ onion   seasoning to taste
1 tablespoon cornflour

Method

Chop onion and fry in margarine until cooked. Add curry powder, stock and pieces of pheasant. Simmer gently for 10 minutes. Thicken with cornflour mixed with a little water. Chop eggs into tiny pieces and stir into curry. Season and serve on a bed of rice.

Pheasant and Prawn Pastries

¾ lb. cooked pheasant   2 oz flour
½ onion   ¼ pint milk
¼ lb. peeled prawns   seasoning to taste
2 oz butter   8 large pastry cases

Method

Chop onion and fry in butter, stir in flour and gradually add milk making a thick white sauce. Add chopped pheasant and prawns and season to taste. Fill pre-cooked pastry cases and pop into hot oven for 10 minutes before serving.

Pheasant Baked Apples

4 large cooking apples
½ lb. pheasant, diced
2 dessertspoons raisins

2 oz. chopped walnuts
2 tablespoons whipped cream

Method

Bake apples and leave to cool. Scoop out the apple and mix all ingredients together leaving cream to last. Put back into apple skins and serve cold.

Pheasant Mayonnaise

cooked pheasant
homemade mayonnaise
2 or 3 pinches of curry powder

black bread
seasoning to taste
paprika

Method

Chop up cooked pheasant. Decide how much mayonnaise you need for the amount of pheasant you have. Mix the curry powder into it then fold in the meat. Season to taste. Place mixture on top of black bread and sprinkle over paprika.

Pheasant and Sweetcorn

½ lb. cooked pheasant
8 oz. sweetcorn
2 oz. margarine
1 small onion
½ clove garlic

½ lb. rice
1 oz. grated carrot
seasoning to taste
cayenne pepper

Method

Chop garlic and onion, fry with carrot in margarine until cooked. Add pieces of pheasant and a pinch of cayenne pepper. Season to taste. Cook rice and mix all ingredients together with sweetcorn. Serve hot or cold.

RABBIT

Rabbit and Noodles

¾ lb. cooked rabbit
¼ lb. bacon
1 small onion
½ lb. noodles

2 oz. margarine
6 oz. sweetcorn
¼ pint double cream
seasoning to taste

Method

Slice onions and cut up the bacon. Fry these in the margarine. Chop up meat and mix these ingredients together. Add sweetcorn and cooked noodles. Put into an oven-proof dish, season to taste and pour over the double cream. Place in pre-heated oven at 350°F for 15 minutes before serving.

Stuffed Potatoes

¾ lb. cooked rabbit
¼ lb. cooked ham
1 onion
¼ pint milk
2 oz. margarine

2 oz. flour
½ teaspoon mixed herbs
½ teaspoon ground black
pepper
8 large potatoes

Method

Bake potatoes then scoop them out. Mash well and place back in skin making a deep nest. Chop onion and fry in margarine, sprinkle over flour and gradually add milk making a thick sauce. Stir in chopped rabbit pieces and ham. Add mixed herbs and ground pepper. Put mixture into potatoes and serve with a green salad.

Curried Rabbit

1 lb. cooked rabbit
1 small onion
2 oz. margarine
2 dessertspoons of curry
powder

1 oz. cashew nuts
1 oz. sultanas
¼ pint rabbit or chicken stock
2 oz. flour

Method

Chop onion and fry in margarine. Stir in curry powder and then add stock and pieces of rabbit. Simmer for 15 minutes then stir in nuts and sultanas, thicken with flour. Serve on a bed of rice.

Rabbit Cheese

½ lb. cooked rabbit   ruskoline
¼ lb. cheddar cheese   4 tablespoons milk
¼ teaspoon paprika   fat

Method

Mince rabbit and grate cheese. Mix these two ingredients together and add paprika. Shape into little balls, dip in milk and roll in ruskoline. Drop these into deep hot fat for a few seconds and serve with a dressed salad.

Rabbit in Tomato Sauce

¾ lb. cooked rabbit   1 tablespoon sugar
½ onion   2 oz. margarine
1 teaspoon dried mint   1 tablespoon flour
4 large skinned tomatoes   seasoning to taste
¼ pint tomato juice

Method

Chop onion, fry in margarine add mint, tomatoes, tomato juice, sugar and pieces of rabbit. Season and simmer for 10 minutes. Use flour mixed with a little water to thicken and serve on a bed of rice.

Rabbit Vegetables

¾ lb. cooked rabbit   2 oz. margarine
1 carrot   ¼ pint rabbit or chicken stock
2 pieces of celery   2 or 3 drops soya sauce
1 small onion
½ lb. bamboo shoots

Method

Slice carrot, celery and onion and fry for 2 minutes in the margarine. Add the stock and cooked meat. Simmer for 20 minutes. Mix in the bamboo shoots and soya sauce, heat through and serve.

SALMON

Salmon Pie

¾ lb salmon (flaked)
2 oz red pepper
2 oz green pepper
1 small onion
½ clove garlic

2 oz margarine
2 oz flour
½ pint milk
2 lbs mashed potatoes
seasoning to taste

Method

Melt margarine in pan and fry the chopped onion, garlic and peppers. Stir in flour and gradually add milk making a thick sauce. Mix in the salmon season and place in oven-proof dish. Cover with mashed potatoes, and put into oven pre-heated at 375°F for ½ hour before serving.

Salmon Cakes

¼ lb cooked salmon
½ onion
1 oz margarine
½ teaspoon lemon juice

4 oz mashed potatoes
1 egg
2 oz breadcrumbs
seasoning to taste

Method

Chop onion into as small pieces as possible and fry in margarine until cooked. Flake the salmon and mash together with the mixed herbs seasoning, lemon juice and mashed potatoes. Shape mixture into salmon cakes, dip in beaten egg, then roll in breadcrumbs. These are now ready to fry when required.

Salmon Mayonnaise

cooked salmon
homemade mayonnaise
chopped chives

seasoning to taste
black bread

Method

These can be used in the quantities desired. Flake the salmon and mix it into the mayonnaise with the chopped chives. Season to taste and serve on top of black bread.

Salmon Kedgeree

¾ lb. cooked salmon
1 small onion
½ clove garlic
2 oz margarine

1 lb rice
2 hard boiled eggs
seasoning to taste

Method

Chop the onion and garlic and fry in the margarine until cooked. Break the salmon into small pieces taking out any bones. Chop up the eggs and mix all ingredients into previously cooked rice. Season to taste. This can be served hot or cold.

Salmon Mousse

½ lb. cooked salmon
2 oz margarine
2 oz flour
sachet of gelatine

¼ pint milk
2 or 3 drops tabasco
seasoning to taste

Method

Melt margarine and mix in the flour adding milk gradually to make a thick sauce, add tabasco and seasoning. Allow to cool then pound fish before adding to sauce or put all ingredients through the liquidizer. Stir in gelatine (previously dissolved) then pour into mould. Allow a couple of hours to set then turn out into serving dish.

Salmon in Aspic

cooked salmon
asparagus tips
aspic

thin slices of cooked ham
strips of red pepper

Method

Here, you may use the quantities you wish to make an attractive dish. Prepare aspic as in menu 3 and put a little on to your dish to set. Wrap a thin piece of ham around each asparagus tip and arrange on dish. Place pieces of salmon neatly between each roll and decorate with strips or red pepper. Cover with aspic jelly and leave to set. Turn out onto a serving dish and serve with mayonnaise.

VENISON

Venison Rissoles

¾ lb. cooked venison
2 slices brown bread
1 carrot
1 onion
1 egg

½ clove garlic
½ teaspoon mixed herbs
¼ teaspoon oregano
2 oz. breadcrumbs
seasoning to taste
fat

Method

Mince venison, bread, carrot, onion and garlic; add herbs, oregano and seasoning. Shape mixture into the size of rissoles you require. Dip into beaten egg and roll in breadcrumbs. Fry rissoles in hot fat until heated through. If there are more than required, these will keep very well in the deep freeze.

Venison Curry

¾ lb. cooked venison, diced
1 small onion
¾ pint hot water
2 oz. margarine
2 dessertspoons curry powder
(strength according to taste)

8 oz. pineapple
¼ pint beef stock
2 tablespoons cornflour
seasoning to taste

Method

Chop onion and fry in margarine, add curry powder. Fry for 1 minute stirring all the time. Add meat and seasoning. Fry for a few seconds then gradually add stock. Leave simmering for ¾ of an hour. Thicken with cornflour. Cut pineapple into small pieces, mix into curry and serve on a bed of rice.

Venison Fritters

sliced cooked venison (2 or 3 slices per person)
flour
pinch of salt
fat

Method

Put some flour and salt in bowl and gradually add cold water until you have a very thick paste. Dip venison slices into batter and fry in hot fat. This can be done in a deep fat pan or in a shallow pan, frying on both sides. Serve with chutney and fried chips.

Venison and Peppers

¾ lb. cooked venison
1 medium size onion
½ green pepper
½ clove of garlic
½ red pepper

2 tablespoons flour
2 oz. margarine
¼ pint stock
seasoning to taste

Method

Chop onion, peppers and garlic and fry in margarine. When cooked sprinkle over flour and stir briskly, gradually adding stock. Dice meat and add to mixture, simmer gently for 5 minutes stirring frequently. Season to taste and serve with rice.

Venison and Spaghetti

½ lb. long spaghetti
1 lb. cooked venison
½ clove garlic
1 small onion
1 small tin tomato puree
2 oz margarine

2 oz. sugar
¼ pint stock
½ teaspoon mixed herbs
2 oz cheddar cheese
seasoning to taste

Method

While cooking spaghetti in salted boiling water, chop onion and garlic and fry in margarine until cooked. Mince meat and add to fried ingredients. Stir in tomato puree, sugar and mixed herbs and continue to fry for a few seconds. Gradually add stock and seasoning to taste. Strain spaghetti and mix all ingredients together. Put in serving dish and grate cheese over the top.

Veniburgers

½ lb. cooked or uncooked
   venison
1 small onion
2 oz pork fat
2 oz bread

½ teaspoon mixed herbs
1 small egg
½ clove garlic

Method

Put all ingredients through mincer, adding mixed herbs and seasoning to minced meat. Bind with beaten egg, shape mixture into burgers and fry when required.

PATENT BISCUIT MACHINE

ROBINSONS BRISTOL.

235

Some Final Tips

All menus serve four generous helpings and in some cases a little more. Temperatures are in Farenheit, therefore below is a chart of equivalents.

Farenheit	Centigrade	Gas
225	110	¼
250	120	½
275	140	1
300	150	2
325	160	3
350	180	4
375	190	5
400	200	6
425	220	7
450	230	8
475	240	9

Wholemeal Bread   (Makes 2 small loaves or 1 large)

¾ lb. wholemeal flour (do not sieve)
¾ lb. plain white flour (sieved)
3 teaspoons of castor sugar
3 teaspoons of salt
¾ pint warm water
1 sachet (¾ oz.) dried yeast

Method

Take ¾ pint warm water and stir in 1 teaspoonful of the sugar. Sprinkle yeast on top and leave for about ½ hour in a warm place, until it is nice and frothy (this will rise better in a plastic bowl or jug). Then mix this into the remaining ingredients and knead well. Place in a large greased bread tin or two small tins and leave in a warm place to rise to double its size. This takes about 1 hour. Put in a pre-heated hot oven at 400°F for about ½ hour. When ready it should sound hollow when tapped on the bottom, and be a nice golden brown on top. Cool on a rack.

Cranberry Sauce

½ lb. Cranberries
½ lb. granulated sugar
¼ pint water

Method

Put sugar and water in pan and heat slowly dissolving sugar. Add berries and boil for 2 or 3 minutes then reduce heat and simmer for a further 10 minutes. This can be served hot or cold.

Redcurrant Jelly

4-6 lbs. redcurrants. Put through a muslin bag. Add 1 lb. granulated sugar to every pint of currant juice. Bring to boil very slowly and boil for 5 minutes. Skim and put into jars.

Stock

beef or chicken bones
1 carrot
1 onion
1 teaspoon mixed herbs
seasoning to taste

Method

Put either beef or chicken bones into pan and cover with water. Chop up carrot and onion and add to pan. Add herbs and seasoning, bring to boil and simmer for 1-2 hours. Strain and leave in bowl to cool. Remove excess fat from top when cold.

Lemon Biscuits

4 oz. plain flour
2 oz. margarine
2 oz. castor sugar
½ beaten egg
½ teaspoon lemon essence

Method

Cream margarine and sugar, add flour and mix together with the beaten egg and essence. Knead and roll out. Cut into rounds and prick with fork. Bake in oven pre-heated at 400°F for 10 minutes until golden brown. Cool on rack.

Mayonnaise

¼ pint oil
½ teaspoon mustard (dried)
½ teaspoon sugar (castor)
1 dessertspoon vinegar or lemon juice
2 egg yolks or 1 whole large egg

Method

Mix all ingredients except for oil, then beat briskly or mix in a mixer or blender adding the oil, drop by drop, until the mayonnaise thickens. Then oil can be added in a continuous stream as long as the stream is kept thin. Season to taste.

I usually make double the quantity and keep what is not needed in an air-tight jar in the fridge.

Conversion Table

British measures are larger than standard American measures which are as follows:

1 American Cup	= 8 fl. oz.
	= 4/5 of a B.S. cup
16 American tablespoons	= 1 American cup
3 American teaspoons	= 1 American tablespoon
	= 4/5 of a B.S. tablespoon
1 American pint	= 16 fl. oz.
	= 4/5 of an Imperial pint

Table of Handy Weights and Measures

	approx. weight of 1 level cup
Flour	5 oz.
Sugar, caster or granulated	8 oz.
Sugar, demarara	7 oz.
Sugar, icing	5 oz.
Fresh breadcrumbs	3 oz.
Currants	8 oz.
Sultanas	6 oz.
Jam	14 oz.
Fat, dripping or margarine	¾-1 lb.